SOUND THE ALARM!

A Warning to the British Nations

by

A.K. Chesterton

CANDOUR

The A.K. Chesterton Trust

2012

This booklet was first printed and published by the Candour Publishing Company in 1954.

This edition is *The A.K. Chesterton Trust Reprint Series* No. 6

Printed & Published 2012

ISBN 978-0-9564669-6-9

The A.K. Chesterton Trust, BM Candour, London, WC1N 3XX, United Kingdom.

Website: www.candour.org.uk

As with the original edition, this booklet is dedicated to our great benefactor and patriot, Robert Key Jeffery.

R.K. Jeffery, 1870 - 1961.

Foreword

The text of this booklet originally appeared in A.K. Chesterton's *Candour* newsletter, and then in booklet form in August 1954. It was the first of a three volume *Sound The Alarm* series.

It was therefore the first 'shot across the bow' to our treacherous ruling class from the newly formed League of Empire Loyalists.

The fact that the L.E.L. ultimately failed in their attempt to awaken the British people to the loss of their Empire does not matter overmuch. It is, after all, better to have fought and lost than not to have fought at all. The spirit of the L.E.L. lives on, and *Candour* continues to be published.

The battle for the Empire was lost, but the battle to awaken the British people to the ever growing threat still continues.

We are not beaten yet.

Colin Todd

The A.K. Chesterton Trust
September 2012

CANDOUR *the British Views Letter*

B Y shrewd, penetrating comment and complete fearlessness *CANDOUR* exposes the dangers confronting our race and seeks to unite serious-minded Britons all over the world to secure the reversal of policies which are destroying our Imperial heritage.

It supports no political party, believing that all have helped to undermine the British present and betray the British future.

It insists that Dollar Imperialism is as deadly a power as Soviet Communism.

It fights these enemies and their fifth columns in the Empire.

It deserves the support of every patriot.

"*Candour* is a *tour de force*. It may well prove to be a rallying point for sanity and thus produce an enormous effect on the politics of our time." —*A famous Fleet Street Journalist.*

"Your paper deserves its name, and there is not one issue which does not call forth my admiration anew for the principles you stand for and your marvellous ability to give expression to them." —*An outstanding World Figure.*

"Thank you for the courage and perspicacity of *Candour*, which must appeal to anyone having the future of our country and of the white race at heart." —*A former Colonial Administrator.*

"Please accept our appreciation of the great work you are doing in informing the people on such vital matters in these troubled times." —*Information Culturelle Integrale*, Canada.

"You are to be congratulated for the forthright way in which you are getting to grips with the evils that beset our British, Christian communities." —*New Times*, Australia.

"This article (Where Communist Power Lies), written by A. K. Chesterton, M.C., is reprinted from May 21st issue of the British newsletter Candour. Mr. Chesterton, a profound student of world affairs and brilliant journalist, was formerly with the Beaverbrook papers." —*The Canadian Intelligence Service, Supplementary Section.*

(Although the names of the private senders of unsolicited testimonials are withheld, the Editor and staff of CANDOUR *vouch for their authenticity.)*

Per annum (52 issues), 25s. Per half year (26 issues), 13s. Per quarter (13 issues), 7s. 6d.

CANDOUR PUBLISHING COMPANY
42 Dingwall Road, Croydon, Surrey

T H E   V O I C E   O F   R E S U R G E N T   B R I T A I N

The inside front cover of the 1954 booklet.

WHY THIS BOOKLET?

The age of vast empires is not dead. Two of them - the Empire of the Dollar and the Empire of the Kremlin - today command the world. The world on that account is spiritually the poorer. Those who control these huge concentrations of power unceasingly strive to bring the whole of mankind within the scope of international despotism. The British Empire, at whose expense they flourish, does not meet the menace by obligingly crumbling into nothingness. It is necessary for the British peoples and for the world that the British Empire should remain and revive.

This booklet is intended to serve a dual purpose. It will introduce new readers to the policy of *Candour*, the British Views-letter, which espouses the British Imperial cause. Indeed, its contents are the substance of articles published by *Candour*. The second purpose is to explain the motives which have led to the formation of the League of Empire Loyalists, a devoted band of patriots pledged to serve the British future by maintaining a relentless opposition to internationalists intent upon enslaving the world through Communism or through Debt.

Sound the Alarm is dedicated to R. K. J., the animator and inspirator of this new movement.

A.K.C.

EMPIRE IN DISRUPTION

The British Empire is disintegrating. Whoever denies that fact is a fool or a knave. Should objection be taken to such strong language, the answer is that the vogue of the understatement, a quite recent pose, covers with precision the period of our national decline. Great Britain and its world system amounted to something in the days when Britons spoke their minds.

History has never known anything quite as strange as the spectacle of a mighty Empire dissolving itself almost without protest.

In the lifetime of many of us there has twice been witnessed the immolation of the flower of our manhood : millions of gay, brave, unassuming young Britons have been flung into battle to suffer death, wounds, tropical illness, or at best the eating away of their youth—for what purpose? They believed it was for their country. But they were wrong. It was for the eclipse and ruin of their country. In what dictionaries should one search for gentle, soothing words with which to convey what one thinks of that betrayal?

In describing the betrayal of our country, and the betrayal of all the British countries overseas, the present writer has a burning urge to tell his fellow-countrymen, in prose as biting as he can command, about the all-out attack on the British Empire and on Christendom itself which so few of them even perceive to be taking place.

* * * *

In place of the British Empire, there arises the Empire of the United States. We have no quarrel on that account with the American people, who are entitled to whatever their dollars can buy. Our quarrel is with our own abject leadership, of whatever party, which has supinely allowed the Dollar Empire to grow fat at our expense, crowding us off the stage of history.

When we are tied to the United States financially and economically to the extent that we are now tied to her diplomatically and militarily - the development so devoutly desired by Mr Butler - our Realm will become a mere husk, a facade to disguise the fact that Queen Elizabeth and her people are no longer sovereign in their own lands. We shall be in everything but name the subjects of a cabal of Wall Street financiers.

Indeed, British power is being, or has already been, smothered by her rival over huge portions of the earth's surface. But the vast majority of people in the British world, or what is left of the British world, affect not to notice their national and imperial eclipse. They mouth comforting platitudes about "democracy", "the free world", "the United Nations",   " N.A.T.O.", "the European Defence Community", "the International Bank", and the rest, with never a thought that these are power-agencies of the New York Money Trust, which seeks the federation of the nations of the world that it may rule over them as firmly as it rules over the United States Government.

The British people do not know, because no newspaper has dared to tell them, that what they call "American generosity", in the shape of American aid, is in fact the price extracted from the taxpayers of the United States for the establishment of the world-wide Dollar Empire.

And the Dollar Emperor is certainly not President Eisenhower.

* * * *

Really well-informed Americans know that their own national sovereignty is as much in jeopardy as is our own or that of any of the other grand, historic old nations of Europe. They know that their institutions, national and international, are more or less at the mercy of the International Money Trust, and that great office is accorded only to those who have no doubt where exclusively to look for guidance. Some Americans are even aware that, although Communism is unquestionably trying to undermine the fabric of our society, it is their own Government which smooths the path for the amazing international oligarchy in their midst by pursuing a barely concealed policy of destroying and supplanting our Empire. When percipient Americans make this discovery, surely Britons ought not to look the other way. As one of them put it: "Your issues are our issues, your fight our fight."

The Secret Axis

Should all this seem surprising to some readers, the reason beyond all doubt is that their eyes are fixed on Moscow as the sole source of danger. They have not yet been able to accept the truth that there is a power superior to Communism and Capitalism which frequently uses one or other, and sometimes both, for ends which, were they to be widely enough known, mankind would not for a moment tolerate. This power - let us call it for convenience the International Money Trust - is hostile to concepts such as national frontiers, pride of race, the independence and rich diversity of men, its hostility being based on the knowledge that the spiritual qualities which these concepts enshrine impede its attempts to set up world socialism under a world government—in other words, its own government — and that they contain the ever-present threat of revolt against its authority.

* * * *

The immediate pretext used for the setting-up of so wide-ranging and exclusive a network of power is the Russian menace. There is no desire on our part to underestimate the seriousness of that menace, which Roosevelt, Morgenthau, Hiss and Co. were so determined should be admitted into the heart of Europe, with consequences now only too apparent.

The vileness of Soviet tyranny never impinged upon the innocent Rooseveltian mind. If it ever impinged upon the minds of his masters, who are still in effective control of the United States, they did not let it deter them from trying to do a deal with the Kremlin. Although for some reason not explained the negotiations for the deal were broken off as early as December, 1945 they went far enough to result in the virtual carving up of the world by Moscow and New York. What is more, should circumstances be propitious, the Money Power would reopen discussions tomorrow for the ruthless completion of that betrayal.

"Protection Racket"

The point which has to be made, however, is that if it be Soviet policy to overthrow the West by force of arms rather than by subversion, the offensive would surely have been taken when there were no more than half a dozen battle-worthy divisions to stand athwart the path of the two hundred Russian divisions massed behind the Elbe. Is it conceivable that the adroit strategists of the Soviet Union would wait for the building up of Western strength before striking? Or are they such simple-minded fellows that the idea of being ringed about in time of war by American atom-bomber bases appeals to the Russian twilight in their souls?

The conclusion is inescapable that the Soviet menace is being used as part of an elaborate conspiracy to reduce the historic nations of Europe to economic impotence and political servitude, and to steal from them the fruits of their long and splendid labours overseas.

As long as the Money-Power is situated in New York and dictates policy to Washington, using the mighty resources of the United States to oust Britain from her world status and make her a financial and political dependency, then so long must we oppose the American nation which allows Wall Street such dominion. If the Devil and the children of the Devil manage to involve us in yet another war, then naturally we shall range ourselves on the American side, because that is inherent in our situation and would be the choice of our hearts as well as of our heads. But to surrender our sovereignty to Wall Street under American duress is a course of action which at all costs we must resist.

* * * *

In my *Truth* days I once wrote an article suggesting the formation of a body called the League of Empire Loyalists. Its function would be to fight against the internationalisation - that is, the destruction - of the British nations and of the great world system known as the British Empire.

Unfortunately a periodical dependent for its existence upon advertisers and newsagents cannot sponsor a political movement of that kind without placing itself in jeopardy, and the interest aroused by the article at home and overseas could not be canalised. Now, however, the League has been created through the agency of *Candour*. It will soon come into action.

LEAGUE OF EMPIRE LOYALISTS

The tendency everywhere to play down the British *motif* exists because Britain has lost faith in herself and in the star of her nationhood. Let that faith be rekindled and we shall become again a great power, second to none in our influence for good.

If the League of Empire Loyalists develops sufficient dynamism at home, its impulses must radiate in all directions to put heart into our kinsmen over-seas and reawaken in them the knowledge that it is a proud thing to be British.

The proposal is not to create a new political party, but to organise public opinion so as to force upon existing parties policies favourable to national and imperial survival in place of the present policies of national and imperial eclipse.

Make Your Views Count!

Organisation, I suggest, ought not to be top-heavy and elaborate: it should require no large bureaucracy at the centre, but should be kept as loose and flexible as possible. Once the basic principle is understood, the members throughout the country and all over the British world will be able to take and sustain the initiative. Working singly or in groups, according to their preference, their first task must be to keep a vigilant watch in their own constituencies upon Members of Parliament and other public men, to discourage in them their present certitude that the one interest they can safely neglect is the national interest. When internationalist doctrines are expounded on national platforms, the resultant nation-wide protest will very soon compel the politicians, most of whom are careerists and time-servers, to face the realities of an awakened national spirit.

* * * *

Had a formidable movement of this kind been in existence in 1945 we could not have lost the peace. The United States, instead of waxing great in power at our expense by feeding us with doles and reducing us financially and militarily to satellite status, would today be treating us with circumspection, as allies to be courted rather than as a spent force to be bulldozed into compliance.

Had there been strong branches in Australia and New Zealand, for example, the notorious Anzus treaty, designed to remove these British nations from the British orbit, would never have been signed.

Had there been strong branches in Canada, the separatist policies of Mackenzie King and St. Laurent would have been impossible.

Had there been strong branches in South Africa the futile and craven United Party would never have dared to betray its cause by admitting republicans to membership.

As the League gains in strength it will give particular attention to stopping the rot in the colonial field. The British in India won the warm affection and loyalty of the great warrior tribes and enjoyed the trust of the vast masses of the peasantry.

We were driven out because we disdained to capitalise for political purposes this super-abundant goodwill, but allowed bunches of frenetic babus and pseudo-sophisticates an absolute monopoly of political propaganda and action. Had there been in the British world an adroitly-managed League of Loyalists, it could have acted in the default of the Government of India by organising against Congress the profound pro-British sentiments, not only of the princes whom we betrayed, but of almost the entire population.

Make Yourself Heard!

The same thing could have been done, perhaps could still be done, in the Sudan, where the British Government has again abandoned without a struggle its most priceless asset - the respect and admiration for Britain of the Sudanese people. It may well be that the revival of the British spirit would itself lead everywhere to a revival of loyalty towards Britain. That spirit in decay, however, can lead only to desertion and disintegration.

The first task of the League must be to face the deadly internationalism which makes progressive inroads upon our national sovereignty, and to send it reeling back with a bloody nose. To do that would be to offer battle to the greatest conspiracy of vested interests ever incubated, a task of immense difficulty, and one appallingly complicated by the ease with which the small group of those who seek world power are able to palm off on the masses a spurious idealism which equates internationalism with the brotherhood of man, whereas its true equation is with the enslavement of man.

* * * *

To get our first clear, authentic glimpse of the policy that is relentlessly being pursued in that conspiracy of vested interests, we have to travel back to the Atlantic Charter meeting. This is what President Roosevelt said to Mr Churchill: "Of course, after the war, one of the pre-conditions of any lasting peace will have to be the greatest possible freedom of trade. No artificial barriers. As few favoured economic agreements as possible. Markets open for healthy competition. . . . Those Empire trade agreements are a case in point."

Churchill fought back. "Mr President," he said, "England does not propose for a moment to lose its favoured position among the British Dominions. The trade that has made England great shall continue, and under conditions prescribed by England's Ministers."

"You see," replied Roosevelt, "it is along in here somewhere that there is likely to be some disagreement between you, Winston, and me." The argument, lasting some days, ended with Churchill's despairing outburst: "Mr President, I believe you are trying to do away with the British Empire."

Well, there was no doubt about that, except in as far as only the voice belonged to Roosevelt. The brains belonged to Baruch, Morgenthau, Frankfurter, Lehmann, Lilienthal and the other members of the international financial caucus. They had the principle written into every Congressional economic enactment, beginning with lend-lease, and their agents, in the guise of Marshall Aid administrators, later arrived in Europe to stampede us into a progressive acceptance of its implications. Sir Winston has lived to see it all work out, but he gives way no more to lamentations. He seems, instead, to be saying with Bishop Blougram: "I soberly acquiesce." There is - let us be quite clear about this - no question of treasonable intent on his part. The explanation may be no more than that it is always difficult for politicians to believe in the finality, or even the occurrence, of national disaster as long as they themselves have the sensation of steering the ship. Sir Winston, after all his brave words, now presides over the liquidation of the British Empire, but so potent is the alchemy of his mind that no doubt he persuades himself that the process is really one of wafting the Empire to the sunlit uplands of his wartime imagining.

The same excuse, however, cannot serve for some of his followers, who give every appearance of working for the abrogation of our national sovereignty as their supreme political objective.

17

Many indeed have been the occasions when the nation has been in sore need of a League of Empire Loyalists to keep close scrutiny on the attitude of its own public men.

1917 - AND ALL THIS

When, at the Geneva Conference, Chou En-lai, representing Red China, arose to tell Dulles, Eden and Bidault to their faces that the Western nations must clear out of Asia, there could have been few present who did not hear the flurry of chickens coming home to roost - chickens bedraggled and moulting, but of a size so stupendous that they could not fail to be identified. The only difficulty, perhaps, was to decide the question of their primogeniture.

As a start must be made somewhere, I would suggest that the trouble began in 1917, when the first Lord Reading (Rufus Isaacs) crossed the Atlantic to arrange with his fellow-racials for Great Britain to receive a loan of £1,000,000,000, which she was to repay *on demand and in gold*. As she did not happen to possess that amount of gold, or anything like it, one can readily understand the pressures to which she was subjected - pressures applied with what can only be described as a diabolical foresight. As a result of one such pressure, the British Government refused to renew the Anglo-Japanese alliance, which had been not only a pillar of world stability but a vital British interest.

Had we possessed leaders with sufficient stamina to defy the master usurers, or a patriotic League strong enough to make itself felt, how much more fortunate would have been the sequence of events. We may be quite sure that the renewal aid nurturing of the Japanese Alliance would have made impossible the present spectacle of an arrogant Chinese Foreign Minister serving us with notice to quit the scenes of our labours.

Anything for a Quiet Death

Thirty years later another British Government, this time a government glowing with a sense of its own rectitude, took a further decisive step towards bringing the Eastern - and with it the Western - world to ruin. It liquidated our Indian Empire. What had been a citadel of strength and a guarantor of peace over a vast area became at one stroke a breeding-ground of potential anarchy and the sounding-board for Mr Nehru, adopting the ludicrous pose of an Archangel of Light, to issue directives well calculated to make a shambles of the rest of Asia.

There were swift and dire consequences. We lost Ceylon. We surrendered Burma to chaos. We immensely weakened our position in Malaya. We facilitated the theft of our oil industry and sphere of interest in Persia. We sowed the seeds of the notorious Anzus treaty. That the whole force of American pressure was behind this orgy of surrender cannot be doubted, but the really alarming fact is that no such pressure was needed to set the ghastly thing in motion. The British Socialist Party seemed to entertain the extraordinary thesis that the immemorial power-drives and struggles for survival between peoples had come to an end throughout the world the moment "nice little Mr Attlee" became Prime Minister of Great Britain.

Years of whining and whimpering in innumerable Trade and Labour Councils - unopposed by any organised patriotic opinion - had induced in the new rulers and their sycophants a masochistic frenzy never before known in these islands, but now embracing every party and completing the rot at the core of Churchillian Conservatism.

Orgy of Betrayal

Nor did the British action in Asia stop at self-betrayal. Holland had turned over the whole of her shipping to us during the war, yet for long we denied her the use of her own ships to send troops to rescue Indonesia from the puppet government left behind by the Japanese. At the same time the lamentable Earl of Mountbatten, who later was to rush in where that splendid Briton, Lord Wavell, had disdained to tread and act as midwife to Nehru's India and Jinnah's Pakistan, performed for the Dutch the historic disservice of recognising the Indonesian rebels as a responsible party fit to negotiate terms with the Dutch Government. Similarly General Gracey, sent to liberate Indo-China, was given a directive so crippling that the opportunity he could have afforded France to reassume full authority was flung away - and flung away in accordance with the deliberate policy of the Roosevelt-Stalin axis, of which the Attlee Government was the enthusiastic stooge.

Now we behold the fruits of that unprecedented orgy of betrayal. Where the momentum of the old British administration has not yet run its course there is still some cohesion. Elsewhere there is bewilderment, illimitable corruption and the shadow of doom. France has fought desperately to ensure her own political defeat in Indo-China. And at Geneva, while the "Great Powers" gave him a respectful hearing, Chou En-lai ordered them to quit what little they have left in Asia.

These home-coming chickens are of the British breed. But there are also American chickens, still larger and more bedraggled, which are returning to roost. The Roosevelt and early Truman administrations were the true creators of Red China. Ringed round with pro-Communist advisers, among them actual Communist agents, and with avowed pro-Russian policies - policies no doubt fashioned by the Red financiers in Wall Street - these enemies of Christendom betrayed Chiang Kai-shek as they betrayed so many of their allies and as they betrayed Western civilisation itself by admitting the Tartar hordes into the heart of Europe. Roosevelt, who was either one of history's most sinister villains or one of her most disastrous clowns, tried to force Chiang to admit Communists to his government, an almost certain method of expediting the Communist march to power.

After Roosevelt died, Truman - or Baruch and the Kuhn, Loeb gang, whichever you please - sent Marshall to continue the pressure on Chiang, while on the Lattimore level the Wall Street and State Department Reds were busy undermining Chiang's regime, softening it up for Mao's victory, which Roosevelt had already assured by double-crossing Nationalist China in a secret agreement with Stalin about future dispositions in Manchuria. Americans, as they received reports of Chou En-lai's speeches at Geneva, must surely have had long, deep thoughts about Roosevelt, Hopkins, Marshall and the whole Red-operated apparatus of their wartime and immediate post-war regimes.

* * * *

Side by side with the American pro-Russian policies, revealed in the notorious memorandum Marshall took with him to Quebec, were the American anti-British and anti-European policies, framed to reduce our power, weaken our sovereignty and destroy our empires and overseas spheres of influence, preparatory to their annexation by the Dollar Barons.

These policies persist, but an angry American uprising has put an end, at any rate for the time being, to the identification of the United States Government with Communist aggrandisement. Instead, advantage has been taken of the international ferment to consolidate "American" power over the non-Communist world in Europe and Australasia and to build up in Asia a huge Wall Street vested interest which pays far bigger dividends than the former secret accord with Moscow. More American technicians and advisers are now in Pakistan, for instance, than there ever were British officials in that country.

Even more significant was President Eisenhower's declaration of the United States interest in Indo-China, which was not to help its French ally but to maintain a free trading area for Japan, now an American colony and repository of many billions of dollars invested there by Kuhn, Loeb and the other New York international lending houses. Yet now that this part of the Dollar Empire is threatened, the Lords of Cosmopolis, through their governmental agents, not only force upon France the relinquishment of her sovereignty in Indo-China, but demand that Frenchmen fight and die for a cause which, so far as France is concerned, no longer exists.

Where in history can one look for a comparable blend of cynicism, impudence and self-interest? The Money Power, now sure of itself, has thrown off all restraint. It treats the nations of the world as cattle. It will not thus treat us when the League of Empire Loyalists throughout Britain and the Empire begins to provide a lead for the patriots of all Christian nations, large and small.

TRUTH ABOUT COMMUNISM

Critics of *Candour's* stand for the national sovereignty of the British peoples against incessant American pressures always base their argument on the supposition that such resistance must aid the Soviet Union. They find incomprehensible our assertion that the opposite is the truth, that as the breaking down of normal tissues provides the conditions favourable for malignant growth, so does every impairment of the principle of nationhood make us the more vulnerable to the cancer of Communism. The belief that the United States affords protection against this danger, whatever may be its momentary truth, is historically false, and it is false not only because America seeks to break down healthy national cells as part of her nominal anti-Soviet policy but also because the Communist cancer was incubated, not in Moscow, but in New York.

Let doubters read with close attention the sixth of President Wilson's Fourteen Points, presented in an address to Congress in January, 1918 : —

"The evacuation of all Russian territory and such a settlement of all questions affecting Russia as will secure the best and freest co-operation of the other nations of the world in obtaining for her an unhampered and unembarrassed opportunity for the independent determination of her own political development and national policy and assure her of a sincere welcome into the society of free nations under institutions of her own choosing; and, more than a welcome, assistance also of every kind that she may need and may herself desire. The treatment accorded Russia by her sister nations in the months to come will be the acid test of their goodwill, of their comprehension of her needs as distinguished from their own interests, and of their intelligent and unselfish sympathy."

That was a most amazing piece of special pleading. As American public opinion, then as now, was wedded to the system of private enterprise, it is clear that in thus furthering the cause of the bloody-handed, anti-Christian revolutionary terrorists President Wilson was not speaking for the American people.

For whom, then, did he speak? The answer is - for the men who plotted and financed the revolution, men who - so far from being the horny-handed sons of toil of the popular imagination - were the international financiers at the heart of the New York Money-Trust. Prominent among them were Jacob Schiff, the Warburg Brothers, Otto Kahn and some of the European affiliates of their international banking firm of Kuhn, Loeb and Co. It was this same complex of interests which had used Wilson to sponsor the creation of the Federal Reserve Board system whereby they gained control over the entire credit mechanism of the United States and became the effective secret government of that country. The same financiers accompanied the President to Versailles, dominated his actions there, and campaigned with the utmost vigour for their "Russian" protégés, then amiably engaged in exterminating their Christian opponents by the millions. I put the word "Russian" in quotation marks, because in truth the makers of the revolution on Russian soil were of the same race as the financial backers of the revolution in Wall Street. These "Russians" using every imaginable kind of fraud to defeat the immigration laws, had swarmed into the United States towards the end of the century, and by slick brains, energy, cohesion and abashless self-confidence had made themselves the biggest and wealthiest pressure group in the land. The British Ambassador, Sir Cecil Spring-Rice, placed on record their power to dictate American policy during the First World War. They were a state within a state, using their host's physical means to serve their own purposes all over the world.

* * * *

When Wilson fell in the great American reaction, the political influence of these Lords of Finance steeply declined, and for many years they were compelled to rely upon other countries - our own among them - to serve their special racial purposes, foremost among them being the nurturing of their Soviet foundling and the preparation of the ground for the rape of Palestine. When Roosevelt came to power in 1932, however, they re-conquered the United States. Incidentally, they made prodigious fortunes out of the New Deal.

The outbreak of the Second World War found them again in a position to take over the secret government of that country and to pursue much the same sinister policy. America did not enter the First World War until Czarist Russia was overthrown, or the Second World War until Hitler attacked Stalin's Russia. Once the Berlin-Moscow axis was shattered, however, the Wall Street cabal swept to its revenge, in the process almost openly organising the United States as a part of the great Finance-cum-Communist conspiracy against Christendom.

Specially protected Reds were placed in key positions, where they evolved the policy which was fulfilled when the Russians were admitted to the heart of Europe and given their heart's desire in the East, and when the decision was taken for the United States to share the post-war world with the Soviet Union - which would assuredly have happened but for Stalin's inexplicable withdrawal from the plot at the end of 1945 - at the expense of Great Britain and the other Western European nations. Innumerable instances of the conspiracy could be furnished, but perhaps none so clear-cut as that provided by General Mark Clark, who tells in his autobiography how, as the Allies pushed back the Germans in Italy, the formidable M. Vyshinsky, with the full knowledge of the U.S. Government, travelled in their wake to try to organise the eventual Bolshevisation of Italy.

From UNO to World Revolution

Even while the war was still being waged the policy-makers of New York, using as tools Red agents such as Alger Hiss and Harry Dexter White, brought into being the United Nations as the basis of a projected super-state and the World Bank as the basis of a projected international credit monopoly. They also created U.N.R.R.A., the two-fold purpose of which was to bolster the economies of the new Soviet satellite states in Eastern Europe, where almost all the relief was distributed, and to finance the illegal migration to Palestine. So blatant had the policy-makers become in the pursuit of their designs that Mr Henry Morgenthau, then Secretary of the United States Treasury, even sent the Russians plates so that they could print their own dollar notes.

No more alarming picture of internationalist power exists than that of the seizure of Palestine, carried through under the direction of international officials armed with the diplomatic immunity which all countries, including our own, were coerced into extending to United Nations and U.N.R.R.A. personnel. There was scarcely a government which was not suborned to play an active part in the infamous proceedings. The picture was first given to the world by General Sir Frederick Morgan, European head of U.N.R.R.A., who related how train-loads of prosperous refugees, with pockets stuffed with money, were allowed out of the Russian-controlled regions to take part in the illegal trek. There had clearly been a bargain between Zionist headquarters and the Kremlin to secure this result. General Morgan was finally dismissed from his post for daring to affirm that U.N.R.R.A. was also functioning as a Communist espionage organisation, his quietus being delivered by New York's La Guardia.

* * * *

So unblushingly has history been falsified before our eyes that most people accept without question the idea that the era of the great American loans began when Washington decided to line up the West against Communism. That is pure fiction. The original proposals included an initial loan of £1,500,000,000 for Russia and Marshall Aid, so far from being an anti-Communist measure, was intended - until Stalin withheld his co-operation - to be fed to countries behind the Iron Curtain.

When the American reaction set in, as it had set in after Wilson's solid support for Russia at Versailles, the master-planners of Wall Street, paying the time but needful woe, concentrated upon building the West into their system through N.A.T.O. and its related bodies, cashed-in upon the seventy billion pounds worth of rearmament orders which followed the outbreak of the Korean War that had been contrived through the deliberate withdrawal of American troops, continued to work for "one world" - their world - and they now await a favourable opportunity of openly reuniting the anti-Christian forces of New York with the anti-Christian Soviet Union.

That policy-objective outlined in Wilson's Point Six has never been dropped. Capitalism and Communism, in terms of power, are merely their twin-mechanisms to destroy the sovereignty of the Christian nations and merge them into the projected super state, where the Money Power will exercise full sway and masterdom through that monopoly of atomic energy which is being sought with such feverish and fiendish persistence.

When the pall of death hung over Hiroshima, the great mass of mankind thought of it in terms of human agony and desolation, but the few - the very few - whose minds took no account of such things thought of it in terms of power - their power. Scarcely had the evil cloud drifted away before the monopolists were seen to have staked their claim to become the masters of this most fearful magic.

It was no accident that atomic energy control in America at once passed into the keeping of the interests which exercised power, not only over the previous master-weapon - which was gold - but also over the United States Government. What is more, had American public opinion not been roused, the secret of nuclear fission would officially have been passed to Moscow, so that if world monopoly were not accorded the policy-makers as a result of their Western power, they might still acquire it through their power in the East. Advance information, together with fissionable material, had already been sent to the Soviet Union by that mysterious White House figure, paid by nobody knows whom, named Harry Hopkins.

Super "Gangster Stuff"

The Congressional decision to ban the sharing of atomic secrets in no way diminished the zeal of the crusade - if that be the word - to secure "international" control of this new source of masterdom. And there was never any doubt as to the financial and racial identity of those who proposed to be the masters.

The plan announced by Mr Bernard Baruch would have given to a small body, no doubt consisting of, or designated by, himself and his cronies of the New York cabal, absolute control over deposits of fissionable material in whatever part of the world they might be located, over their mining, their storage, their processing and their ultimate use. There has never before been witnessed a more blatant or a more outrageous attempt to dominate mankind by cornering the materials of power - power not only over the economies of the nations, but over their actual physical existence.

The grand strategic end was the World State, marshalled by atomic police in service to International Finance.

"Eisenhower's Idea"!

I have written "was," but the plot, unhappily, does not belong to the past: it is perhaps at this moment reaching its greatest intensity of endeavour. Consider this fact. When the Berlin Conference was mooted at Bermuda during the Eisenhower - Churchill meeting, skilled hands were manipulating the strings behind the scenes, with the result that the President flew back to announce to the General Assembly of the United Nations "his" scheme for the establishment of a world bank of atomic energy.

Admiral Lewis Strauss, of the good ship Kuhn Loeb & Co., informed his fellow-countrymen a few weeks ago that President Eisenhower had given long and profound thought to such a project. That is as it may be. What would seem to have more relevance is that twenty-five years ago, when only a Major in the United States Army, Eisenhower made the one and only move of his career which history will describe as brilliant - acting on sheer inspiration, this obscure officer sought and obtained the advice of Mr Bernard Mannes Baruch.

Never was any step so richly rewarded. Baruchian influence later lifted him over the heads of one hundred and fifty of his seniors to place him at the head of the Allied armies in the West. After the War Baruchian influence placed him in cold storage at Columbia University, until the time was ripe for Baruchian power to make him President of the United States. And now Admiral Strauss, present chairman of the U.S. Atomic Energy Commission, has the charming innocence to ask us to believe that it was Eisenhower, the simple soldier, and not his patron and benefactor, who conceived of the idea of a World Atomic Bank. The secret of the masterdom of the Lords of Baruchistan is that they use every sort of camouflage to disguise the fact that they relentlessly pursue purposes which easy-going Christendom imagines long ago to have been dropped.

Something Special

The timing of the Eisenhower announcement and the method of its presentation were designed to carry the suggestion that the World Atomic Bank was all part of the Berlin peace move. Indeed, it was during the Conference that discussions for the Bank's establishment began between the United States and the Soviet Union. Why these two countries should be regarded as the twin foundation-stones of the revived scheme for atomic monopoly has not been explained, nor is it likely to be explainable except in terms of that sinister polarity which I have endeavoured to show. It is sufficient to note that the atomic talks did not falter when the Berlin Conference faltered, or break down when the Berlin Conference broke down. Nor were they affected by any of the U.S.-U.S.S.R. clashes at the Geneva Conference. They were something very special, these talks - something truly supra-national.

Suspended at the moment of writing, they will assuredly be resumed.

Lords Over All

While they are proceeding, Admiral Strauss works overtime, and with an almost comic obsequiousness, to praise the sublime wisdom of President Eisenhower in having initiated them. The propaganda-backing is world-wide. And no wonder. The stakes are immense.

Imagine the industries of all the nations a few years hence driven by atomic energy supplied by the World Atomic Bank, because that is the essence of the proposal. Then imagine the overwhelming disaster to any national economy which, in the event of potential disobedience, would follow the cutting off of such supply.

It is for that power to cut off supplies that the leaders of the International Financial junta work with relentless purpose. Once it is theirs this world in its totality will belong to them. Admiral Strauss, of course, exudes enthusiasm from every pore as he tells mankind of the blessings which will accrue once the plan is accepted. The altruism, the passionate love of their fellow-men, exhibited by the members of the cherubic firm of Kuhn, Loeb & Co. is such as to warm the heart.

The Emperor Baruch, while lending the authority of his own voice to the splendiferous promises of the good Admiral, continues to stress the more rigorous aspect of the plan - control. President Eisenhower's proposal, he told a New York audience - generously giving credit where it was not due - "will be a worthy endeavour if it succeeds in widening peaceful atomic uses", but it could not take the place of "a truly effective, enforceable system of international inspection and control".

Mr Nehru, whatever else may be said of him, at least had the courage to show his awareness of the plot. The American proposals, he pointed out:

"envisage an international control agency which will be set up by the United Nations but will be independent of the world body. This control agency, according to the U.S. proposal, will have guards in the territories of other countries and also power to give or withhold licences to countries and people for purposes of production or research in atomic energy. Such a body will in fact become a super state, maintaining its own guards or army. The proposal means concentration of tremendous powers in the hands of the select body."

What the Indian Prime Minister proclaims today was asserted seven years ago by two British publicists who, working independently of each other, had reached the identical conclusion. One of the publicists was Mr Douglas Reed. The other, if the claim may be made with seemliness, was the present writer.

Both had long been students of the technique used by the Lords of Misrule.

Admiral Strauss would be very scornful of any doubt being cast upon the motives behind the "Plan". He tells us, indeed, that it is intended to allay apprehension about the atomic future. I do not know whose fears it stills. It greatly accentuates my own.

The "Russians", or "Poles", or "Germans" who have conquered America seek also to conquer us. They have already, under cover of our alliance, in large part destroyed the British Empire. That is why *Candour* proclaims the need for a great British revival and a British Declaration of Independence. We are being blinded by the alliance, with its fiction that our destroyers are our protectors.

They are nothing of the kind. They will sell us into slavery as willingly as they will sell into slavery the American people upon whom they now wax fat and whose material resources they use for their own nefarious world-wide purposes. To say, as some say, that in exposing their plans for world dominion we are playing the Kremlin's game is to act as an unconscious agent of Christendom's betrayal.

The tragedy is that although the facts I have narrated are well known to an increasing number of people in the United States, there is almost total ignorance of them in the British world, where even to mention them is to conjure up in sleepy, complacent British minds a sense of the preposterous - and consequently to be adjudged mad.

The facts nevertheless remain facts. Nothing has been written here which cannot be proved. Fortunately the conspiracy has not yet fully succeeded. Whether or not it does succeed depends in large part upon our capacity to warn our fellow-countrymen of their danger, because only the retention of British sovereignty and the restoration of British power can ensure to the world that stability which will save mankind from the appalling tyranny of the proposed all-embracing Centralised Police State.

As things are, our people are lulled by Communist deposits lost at the polls. That is not the kind of Communism we have to fear. Communism is not a movement of poor men, but of rich men - the richest men in the world - and it does not need Communists in the British House of Commons to bring us crashing to the ground.

That aim is achieved by attacking our national sovereignty, in which cause Members of Parliament, forgoing their brains, only too often lead the van.

LEADERSHIP WANTED

Although their heads are undoubtedly confused, the instincts of the mass of British people are not yet decayed. Given forthright British leadership, there could not possibly be found a more essential, a more popular, a more inspiring cause than a national and imperial revolt against all the sinister internationalist enemies who beset us, determined that we shall be transformed from proud Britons (those of us, at least, who are still proud to be Britons) into a cosmopolitan rabble, herded and driven by the leaders of the internationalists who frequently in their own newspapers and meetings proclaim this to be their supreme objective.

The fact that few Parliamentarians dare to espouse the popular cause of Britain is a frightening tribute to the power of the unseen opposition.

Conservatism is so smug, so entrenched in self-esteem, so lacking in conviction or principle, that only an electoral demonstration on a wide enough scale that "patriotism pays", that there really are "votes in it", would call back the Tory hounds from vieing with Labour and Liberal hounds in pursuit of the internationalist hare and send them off upon the worthier course of national survival.

Politics and Bread and Butter

Does this seem too harsh a generalisation about Conservative Parliamentarians? I do not think it is very wide of the mark. Some are better than others, of course, but take them all in all they are a poor, tame, gutless bunch, prepared to be all things to all men, always sheltering behind smooth but meaningless catchwords. One or two have said to me: "My dear fellow, you should realise that we do much better service by not making a public stand. It is in committee that the real work is done and there, we assure you, we make our voices effectively heard."

I was more impressed by that argument three or four years ago than I am now. Although the Empire is falling apart in the flabby, nerveless hands of the Conservatives at as fast a rate as it was given away by the Socialists, there have been only one or two protests from those whom some of us have supposed, too charitably, to be the custodians of the imperial cause. As we are dragged along at the cart's-tail of New York our independence as a nation is being steadily

31

destroyed. We hand over without a murmur our spheres of influence in Greece, Turkey, Egypt, Persia and Pakistan to our supplanters; and if dissident Tories in the privacy of committee are indeed kicking up a row about the perpetual surrender it must be a very decorous row, so decorous as to be completely futile. "Now do be reasonable," they will say to me. "What do you want us to do - break up the Party?" They fail to explain where lies the profit in preserving the Party and losing the Empire.

The truth is that Party warfare today, even more than when Belloc and Cecil Chesterton exposed it, is a pitiful sham-fight. Its moves have become as stylised as the conventions of Chinese drama.

Treason Must Not Pay

The real political issues, thanks to the dewy-eyed enthusiasm of some or the supine defeatism of others of our Members of Parliament, cut across Party-lines and reveal themselves as mere differences of opinion upon the manner and the speed with which we divest ourselves of our age-long national independence, and transfer our terrestrial loyalty to a "higher" authority than Her Majesty the Queen - a junta whose visible members might well be Dulles, Eden, Spaak, Mrs Pandit, Major Salem and Uncle "General China" and all! That adherence to some form of greasy internationalism should have become a shimmering political objective for every British political party is the measure of our fall.

Whether or not a new party would be any better than the old parties, one thing is certain: the nation cannot long continue on its present basis of spiritual treason. Because it is treason, beyond doubt it is treason, to dissipate the heritage of a thousand years; destroy the values which those thousand years have seen created, and prepare to hand over the sovereign right to our obedience to the people who are putting up the money for "World Government " - that is, to the World Governors Designate, the would-be masters of mankind who are indifferent whether their tyranny is implemented by international financial sanctions or by the Arctic labour-camps so long as no such "anachronism" as a sovereign national state is left to challenge the absolutism of their power.

* * * *

On the question of how a national revolt might be organised, and the fruits of victory achieved and preserved, a recent public opinion poll disclosed that a majority of those taking part no longer had confidence in the Conservative

Party, or its leader, to save the British Empire from extinction. It is good to find men and women breaking loose from the hot-house atmosphere of high-pressured propaganda and facing facts. What should they do next?

Nothing is easier than to start a new political party. One man in a room has only to declare himself to be the president or secretary or whatever it may be of such an organisation, and to give it a name, for a new party to exist, even though it may expire the same day. Many dozens, perhaps many hundreds, are born every year. The significant fact, however, is that in our nation of fifty million souls only three parties enjoy electoral support, and of these three one is being inexorably squeezed out of the arena.

Thus the inescapable conclusion is that, though the birth of a political party presents no problem, to nurse it through its teething troubles is perhaps the most difficult task possible to imagine. Most parties, for all practical purposes, are still-born. The infant mortality rate among the rest is about 100 per cent. Here and there a group struggles on in almost total obscurity for a few years, to die without having made the slightest impact on the country's political life.

Those who talk of starting a new party should ask themselves how they propose to secure for it immunity from the common fate. But that does not mean we are without means of defence and counter-attack.

There is no Internationalist Party, yet every party is rotten with internationalism. The reason is that the internationalists have captured all the key positions, including the B.B.C., Chatham House and even the political columns of many newspapers which are supposed in the popular imagination to represent quite a different point of view. I have particularly in mind Mr H. V. Hodson, editor of the *Sunday Times*, Mr Alistair Forbes, political commentator of the *Sunday Dispatch*, and Mr C. S. Melville, diplomatic correspondent of the *Evening News*. These are internationalists serving Conservative newspapers, and surprising though it may seem the vast bulk of Conservative opinion still believes that the Conservative Party is the champion of a sovereign, independent Britain.

Conservatives have not yet realised that it is almost as completely the handmaiden of internationalism as any of its rivals in the amicable shadow-fighting of Westminster.

Now nobody really supposes that in the breasts of the sturdy sons and daughters of Britain resides any exorbitant love of alien influences in their public or commercial life, or that they long for their terrestrial loyalty to be transferred from Her Majesty the Queen to some cosmopolitan cabal functioning as a supranational government in New York or Tel-Aviv. It just happens that small groups of very clever propagandists contrive to misrepresent the prevailing climate of opinion in the image of their own designs. What has to be done, therefore, is to secure a hearing for the authentic voice of Britain. Is there any reason why we should not profit from the example of our adversaries?

This is where the League of Empire Loyalists re-enters the picture. There is being brought rapidly into being an organisation of British patriots which will raise such a hornets' nest under any public man who dares to speak or act against British sovereignty as to put him in fear of his political career.

The organisation will not cut across a patriot's positive political creed: given good faith he can belong to any party or group, or to none. By supporting the proposed vigilance movement he will help to ensure the retention of a country in which to work for the fulfilment of his own beliefs. Men may have legitimate differences of opinion as to how to cultivate their garden, but if in the course of quarrelling about it the garden is filched from under their noises, who but their despoiler profits?

* * * *

The immediate task is the defeat of the enemy and the liberation of the British genius that it may again assume the leadership of mankind, a role that in the long run depends less on quantitative considerations (American dollars or Soviet manpower) than on quality. British morale in the past has been incomparably great. In an age full of the atomic menace, it is certain that the only weapon which can stand up to the atom bomb is the weapon of morale.

The desperate need is unity. The League of Empire Loyalists therefore fights on the sole issue of national and imperial survival. But too much emphasis cannot be placed on the fact that the League, instead of competing against bodies whose aims of social and economic reform require the retention of national sovereignty, can only give them powerful background support and ultimately a vast recruiting ground.

Enough has probably been written to show why, in facing the illimitable dangers which threaten our historic nation, we do not give a more particularised support to constructive policies. When the house is on fire, its occupants - at any rate those of the British breed - do not normally fall out about the rebuilding or the refurnishing until the flames have been put out.

Unfortunately only a few intellectually alert Britons to-day understand that the national house is ablaze.

That is why we have made it our own task to sound the alarm. We seek the help of our fellow-countrymen. Once their ears are reached and their eyes opened, we are convinced their hearts will not fail.

If you agree with the aims of

CANDOUR

you will wish to join

THE LEAGUE OF EMPIRE LOYALISTS

Information and Application Forms may be had from:

The Organising Secretary

LEAGUE OF EMPIRE LOYALISTS

Room 602, Grand Buildings, Northumberland Avenue, London, W.C.2

JOIN WITH US TO PROTECT OUR HERITAGE AGAINST MOSCOW AND WALL STREET—

AS WELL AS AGAINST THEIR FIFTH COLUMNS IN THE BRITISH EMPIRE

AND THE GREATEST DANGER OF ALL WHICH IS THE APATHY OF PUBLIC OPINION AT HOME

The rear inside cover of the 1954 booklet.

About A.K. Chesterton

Arthur Kenneth Chesterton was born at a gold mine where his father was an official in South Africa in 1899.

In 1915 unhappy at school in England A.K. returned to South Africa. There and without the knowledge of his parents, and having exaggerated his age by four years, he enlisted in the 5th South African Infantry.

Before his 17th birthday he had been in the thick of three battles in German East Africa. Later in the war he transferred as a commissioned officer to the Royal Fusiliers and served for the rest of the war on the Western Front being awarded the Military Cross in 1918 for conspicuous gallantry.

Between the wars A.K. first prospected for diamonds before becoming a journalist first in South Africa and then England. Alarmed at the economic chaos threatening Britain, he joined Sir Oswald Mosley in the B.U.F and became prominent in the movement. In 1938, he quarrelled with Mosley's policies and left the movement.

When the Second World War started he rejoined the army, volunteered for tropical service and went through all the hardships of the great push up from Kenya across the wilds of Jubaland through the desert of the Ogaden and into the remotest parts of Somalia. He was afterwards sent down the coast to join the Somaliland Camel Corps and intervene in the inter-tribal warfare among the Somalis.

In 1943 his health broke down and he was invalided out of the army with malaria and colitis, returning to journalism. In 1944, he became deputy editor and chief leader writer of *Truth*.

In the early 1950s A.K. established *Candour* and founded the League of Empire Loyalists which for some years made many colourful headlines in the press worldwide. He later took that organisation into The National Front, and served as its Chairman for a time.

A.K. Chesterton died in 1973.

About *The A.K. Chesterton Trust*

The A.K. Chesterton Trust was formed by Colin Todd and the late Miss. Rosine de Bounevialle in January 1996 to succeed and continue the work of the now defunct Candour Publishing Co.

The objects of the Trust are stated as follows:

"To promote and expound the principles of A.K. Chesterton which are defined as being to demonstrate the power of, and to combat the power of International Finance, and to promote the National Sovereignty of the British World."

Our aims include:

- *Maintaining and expanding the range of material relevant to A.K. Chesterton and his associates throughout his life.*
- *To preserve and keep in-print important works on British Nationalism in order to educate the current generation of our people.*
- *The maintenance and recovery of the sovereign independence of the British Peoples throughout the world.*
- *The strengthening of the spiritual and material bonds between the British Peoples throughout the world.*
- *The resurgence at home and abroad of the British spirit.*

We will raise funds by way of merchandising and donations.

We ask that our friends make provision for *The A.K. Chesterton Trust* in their will.

The A.K. Chesterton Trust has a **duty** to keep *Candour* in the ring and punching.

CANDOUR : To defend national sovereignty against the menace of international finance.

CANDOUR : To serve as a link between Britons all over the world in protest against the surrender of their world heritage.

The A.K. Chesterton Trust Reprint Series

1. Creed of a Fascist Revolutionary & Why I Left Mosley - A.K. Chesterton.

2. The Menace of World Government & Britain's Graveyard - A.K. Chesterton.

3. What You Should Know About The United Nations - The League of Empire Loyalists.

4. The Menace of the Money-Power - A.K. Chesterton.

5. The Case for Economic Nationalism - John Tyndall.

6. Sound the Alarm! - A.K. Chesterton.

7. Six Principles of British Nationalism - John Tyndall.

8. B.B.C. - A National Menace - A.K. Chesterton.

9. Stand By The Empire - A.K. Chesterton.

10. Tomorrow. A Plan for the British Future - A.K. Chesterton.

Other Titles from *The A.K. Chesterton Trust*

Leopard Valley - A.K. Chesterton

Juma The Great - A.K. Chesterton

New Unhappy Lords - A.K. Chesterton

Facing The Abyss - A.K. Chesterton

The History of the League of Empire Loyalists and Candour - McNeile and Black.

All the above titles are available from The A.K. Chesterton Trust, BM
Candour, London, WC1N 3XX, UK

www.candour.org.uk

Printed in Great Britain
by Amazon